the edge

[FAITH in a
precarious place]

Name:

_____

Date:

_____

Destination:

_____

Graphic design by Julie Anderson.
Cover photo © Cathysbelleimage, dreamstime.com

Unless otherwise indicated, all Scripture quotations are taken from the HOLY BIBLE, NEW INTERNATIONAL VERSION © 1972, 1978, 1984 by International Bible Society. Used by permission of Zondervan. All rights reserved.

Published in Gainesville, Georgia, by Praxis Press, Incorporated.

Praxis Press, Inc.
3630 Thompson Bridge Rd. #15-100
Gainesville, GA 30506

www.praxispublishing.com
www.MissionsResources.com

For additional copies of The Edge: Faith in a Precarious Place, see the website or email
info@MissionsResources.com

Printed in the USA

ISBN 978-1-934278-12-3
ISBN 1-934278-12-2

TABLE OF

contents

INTRODUCTION

the edge

Have you ever stood on the edge of something really big?

The Grand Canyon maybe? Or the Atlantic Ocean? Or just anything that made you think, *I am so small and God is so big*?

Or maybe it wasn't an actual physical edge, but something a little more figurative, like a new challenge or new phase of life...the first day of high school? the last day of college? a new job? a new difficulty? or just any situation packed with extreme potential and uncertainty all at the same time.

The Edge.

It can be exciting. It can be scary. It can cause your stomach to do back flips and tempt you to retreat to safer ground. But many times it's exactly where God wants us to be, because that's where we find him.

The edge is where we learn to trust him.

Scripture is full of people who were faced with a choice: a) trust God, or b) make a run for it. The Bible is also packed with promises for those of us who can muster up the faith to choose "a". That's what this whole book is about: choosing to trust God and follow him even when our flesh screams "no!"

It's about choosing faith.

How to use this journal:

This journal is made especially for use during your short term mission trip. There are 10 days of material to be used during your trip, and then an additional 3 days to help ease you back into real life when your trip is over. While on your trip you'll probably be waking up early and staying up late, but making room for some focused time with God each day is vital. God wants to pour his life and love into you, so that you can give it out to others. Don't miss out on all He wants to do in you and through you!

Each day includes:

Scripture to read and think about.
Some days the verses are written out for you, other days you'll dig into your Bible for yourself. Take time to read the key scriptures over a couple of times and really absorb the meaning.

Questions or activities to complete.
The questions and activities given each day will help you to better understand the meaning of the day's scripture and how it applies to your life and ministry.

God wants to pour His life and love into you, so that you can give it out to others.

Space to write.
This book intentionally contains lots of white space for you to journal your answers to each days questions, your thoughts and prayers, and anything you sense the Lord is saying to you. Getting things down on paper can help solidify the work that God is doing in you on your trip.

Daily Debrief.
Answer these questions at the end of the day to help you process your missions experience. If possible, discuss your answers with your teammates.

PRE-TRIP

getting ready to go

There's way more to getting ready for your mission trip than packing your bags. In the weeks before your trip, take some time to do a few or all of the following extra preparations:

Take a mini-retreat.
If possible, plan a day or even just an afternoon away for you and God. Use the time to complete some of the assignments listed here. Spend a lot of time in prayer just asking God how he wants to prepare you for what's ahead.

Read and think about these key scriptures.
Spend time journaling ways you think the truth they contain will apply to you, your team, and your ministry. If you're able, get together with other teammates and share your thoughts.
- Romans 12
- Ephesians 6:10-20
- Isaiah 58:6-12
- Psalm 67
- Philippians 2:1-18

Be purposeful about praying for what's ahead.
- Gather prayer requests from your team mates about things they'd like prayer for as they prepare for the trip.
- Do some research on the location you're going to visit. Do some research on the internet, or talk to others that have been there to find out needs you can be praying about. The book *Operation World* (Johnstone) can be a helpful resource to find out more about where you are going.
- See if your team leader has the names of specific people or ministries you'll be working with in your trip location. Begin

praying for those people. Pray that God would use you to be a blessing to them

---

Start thinking outside your bubble
On your mission trip you'll see up close that not everyone thinks like you, lives like you, looks like you, talks like you, or believes like you. Looking at some of the differences between people and cultures before you go will help prepare you for what's ahead.

- Go to an ethnic restaurant (Taco Bell doesn't count) and order something you've never eaten before—then eat it!
- Talk to someone from another culture. Ask them about what differences they see between American culture and their own.
- If you're going someplace that speaks a language other than your own, learn a few key phrases.

Get the right attitude
There's nothing like the intensity of a mission trip to bring out the best and worst in a person. Start praying about and practicing these attitudes that will be so important in making your trip a success:

- **Selfless:** how can you put other's needs above your own?
- **Servant:** who can you serve today that will take you out of your comfort zone?
- **Flexible:** how patient are you with unexpected changes and obstacles in your day?
- **Teachable:** how ready are you to learn different ways of doing things and looking at situations?

DAY ONE:

not by sight

So we fix our eyes not on what is seen, but what is unseen.
For what is seen is temporary, but what is unseen is eternal.
2 Corinthians 4:18

We live by faith and not by sight.
2 Corinthians 5:7

What if, instead of letting what we see determine what we do, we let our faith be what drives our actions?

Have you ever been standing in a room when the lights went out unexpectedly? All of a sudden you're forced to forego your sense of sight, and resort to feeling your way around the room. A few stubbed toes and bruised shins later, you may actually get to the comfy chair you were aiming for. No doubt about it, sight is a pretty handy ability to have. If you see a big hole in your path, you walk around it. If you see someone swinging a bat at your head, you duck. What we see often determines what we do.

God's word calls to "live by faith and not by sight." What do you think that might mean?

Hebrews 11:1 - Now faith is being source of what we hope for & certain of what we do not see.

What if, instead of letting what we see determine what we do, we let our faith be what drives our actions? Our limited human vision might look at a situation and say, "Ouch, that could be painful and embarrassing," while faith might say, "this could be a great opportunity for God to be glorified." Human perspective might say,

"Let's avoid anything we might fail at," while faith says, "Let's do this and trust God to give us what we need!" *How much of the amazing adventure God has for us have we missed because we chose to look at a situation with our human eyes rather than eyes of faith?*

In what ways do you think God is calling you to "walk by faith and not by sight?"

Think about some of the specific situations you're experiencing on this mission trip and then dissect them a little bit below:

> **Situation #1:**

> **What our sight might tell us:**

> **What faith would say:**

> **Situation #2:**

> **What our sight might tell us:**

> **What faith would say:**

Spend some time praying, asking God to increase your faith, and let *it* be what determines your thoughts, words and actions.

Living by faith and not by sight.

Trusting God's promises more than we trust ourselves.

Attempting huge and impossible things, because we're confident in our huge all-things-are-possible God.

Close your eyes and start walking by faith.

"When the train goes through a tunnel and the world gets dark, do you jump out? Of course not.
You sit still and trust the engineer to get you through."
--Corrie ten Boom

today···

How did you see God at work?

How was your faith challenged?

Who blessed you?

What's something new you learned about your location?

How can you bless others tomorrow?

DAY TWO:

a name you can trust

Some trust in chariots and some in horses,
but we trust in the name of the LORD our God.
Psalm 20:7

The name of the LORD is a strong tower;
the righteous run to it and are safe.
Proverbs 18:10

In his name the nations will put their hope."
Mathew 12:21

Have you ever flipped through one of those baby name books? Pages of names with thousands of meanings? Fortunately for you, your parents probably didn't name you *Quirtsquip*[1], because not only does it sound strange, but it means *Chewing Elk*. And *Acton* may sound kind of cool and unique, but its meaning is *from the Oak Tree Settlement*. Not so bad, but not that great either.

In the days of the Old Testament, names were significant. For the Hebrew, a person's name represented his character or described his nature.[2] So in the Bible, when people saw God do something amazing that showed them more of who He was and what He could do, they often gave Him a new name or title. (see Genesis 22:1-18; Exodus 17:8-15 for examples).

As a child of God, you can confidently put your hope in the fact that God is who He says He is, and that He will prove himself to be exactly that.

Take a look at this list of just a few of the names, titles, and descriptions of God given in Scripture.

Bread of life (John 6:35)
Comforter (Jeremiah 8:18)
My Hope (Psalm 71:5
Wonderful Counselor (Isaiah 9:6)
Faithful and True (Revelation 19:11)
Father (Isaiah 6:8)
A sure foundation (Isaiah 28:16)
Friend (Job 16:20)
Almighty God (Genesis 17:1)
Our Guide (Psalm 48:14)
Our Help (Psalm 33:20)
Hiding Place (Psalm 32:7)
Our Life (Colossians 3:4)
Light of life (John 8:12)
Mediator (1 Timothy 2:5)
Our Peace (Ephesians 2:14)
Prince of Peace (Isaiah 9:6)
Redeemer (Psalm 19:14)
Refuge and Strength (Psalm 46:1)
My help (Psalm 42:5)
My Stronghold (Psalm 18:2)
King of kings and Lord of lords (1 Timothy 6:15)
My support (2 Samuel 22:19)
My Rock (Psalm 18:46)
Defender of widows and orphans (Psalm 68:5)

As a child of God, you confidently put your hope in the fact that God is who He says He is, and that He will prove Himself to be exactly that.

Can you believe who your God is? who He wants to show Himself to be in your life? Not even this list of names can begin to describe how great and awesome He is. Read through the list again, taking time to really think about the meaning, especially of any that stand out to you.

From the list, what names or descriptions of God stood out to you?

How would what your thoughts and actions change if you really lived like you believe God is _____ ?

What makes you nervous or fearful about your mission trip?

What name or description of God speaks to that fear?

Spend some time praying, asking God to squash your fears and explode your faith through experiencing first-hand who He is during your mission trip.

---

[1] meanings found on www.babynames.com
[2] Experiencing God, Henry Blackaby © 1994, Broadman & Holman Publishers, pg 8

What's the problem? Why don't we run to the arms of our all-sufficient God? I think it's because most of us don't really know our God. To know His name is to know Him.
--Kay Arthur, Lord I want to Know You

today...

How did you see God at work?

How was your faith challenged?

What did you enjoy most?

What made you laugh?

How can you bless others tomorrow?

DAY THREE:

eyes to see

Long before Paul ever wrote about living by faith and not by sight, the prophet Elisha was an expert at it.

Read 2 Kings 6:8-23.

The people of Aram were after the people of Israel. Time and time again they made plans to intercept and capture them. Every time the Israelites managed to elude them, because the man of God, Elisha, would warn them of the traps the Aramites were setting.

Sometimes you may feel abandoned, but as followers of Christ, we need to learn to expect much more than we can see.

God had revealed much more to Elisha than the plans of the enemy. When the armies of Aram arrived on a personal mission to capture him, there was no evidence of fear found in Elisha. When the servant ran in frightened, we see exactly why Elisha remained so calm.

Read verses 16-17 again:

"Don't be afraid," the prophet answered. "Those who are with us are more than those who are with them. And Elisha prayed, "O Lord open his eyes so he may see." Then the Lord opened the servant's eyes, and he looked and saw the hills full of horses and chariots of fire all around Elisha."
2 Kings 6:16-17

God's children are never alone. Sometimes you may feel abandoned, but as followers of Christ, we need to learn to expect much more than we can see. When we come to a crossroads or a crisis, we don't have to fear. We can trust. We don't have to freak out and scream, "This is a disaster! My life is over!" we can confidently say, "God somehow has a plan in all this for my good and His glory."

Ask God to give you eyes of faith to see the truth about each situation you face.

The very same conditions that inspire fear are often the very same conditions needed to inspire faith. Any life challenge presents us with a basic choice: fear or faith?
--Joanna Weaver, Having a Mary Spirit

today...

How did you see God at work?

How was your faith challenged?

Why are you thankful?

What was hardest for you?

How can you bless others tomorrow?

DAY FOUR:

not alone

After the death of Moses, Joshua became the new leader of God's chosen people, the Israelites. They had a reputation for being a not-so-easy group of people to lead. Their journey so far had been marked by lots of grumbling and a faith that wavered from day to day, to put it lightly. However, Joshua had stood out from the rest of the crowd. When the leader position opened up, God chose to fill it with Joshua. Moses led them out of slavery in Egypt and up to the edge of the Promised Land they'd been journeying toward for more than 40 years. Now it fell on Joshua to get them in and make it theirs.

Read Joshua 1:1-10.

Let's look more closely at verses written below. As you read these words of God to Joshua, underline any commands God give, and circle any promises.

> *No one will be able to stand up against you*
> *all the days of your life.*
> *As I was with Moses, so I will be with you;*
> *I will never leave you or forsake you.*
> *Be strong and courageous, because you will lead these people to*
> *inherit the land I swore to their forefathers to give them.*
> *Be strong and courageous. Be careful to obey all the law my*
> *servant Moses gave you; do not turn from it to the right or to the*
> *left, that you may be successful wherever you go.*
> *Do not let this Book of the Law depart from your mouth; meditate*
> *on it day and night, so that you may be careful to do everything*
> *written in it. Then you will be prosperous and successful.*
> *Have I not commanded you? Be strong and courageous. Do not*
> *be terrified; do not be discouraged, for the Lord your God will be*
> *with you wherever you go.*
> *Joshua 1:5-9*

What similar phrases do you see repeated throughout these verses?

God was fully aware of Joshua's thoughts and emotions as he stood on the edge of the Promised Land. Considering God's words to Joshua, what do you think Joshua must have been feeling at this point?

Isn't it great to see that when one of His children might be experiencing some fear over the challenge set before him, God doesn't just say, "Suck it up and get moving!" God takes time to speak to Joshua and to reassure him of His presence. It's something we see God do throughout scripture. When he called Abraham, Jacob, Moses, Jehoshephat, Jeremiah, Gideon, Mary and more, Jesus accompanied a call to do something great with a great promise: I AM WITH YOU. The promise of His continual presence seems to be His direct answer to our fears of following where He's sending us. Not only is he sending us to accomplish his purposes, He's going with us to give us everything we need to do it.

> Jesus accompanied a call to do something great with a great promise: I AM WITH YOU.

How is God's presence a comfort and encouragement to you today?

The Bible teaches that we are to do our part by faith and the Spirit will do his part by his power.
--Henry Cloud & John Townsend, How People Grow

today···

How did you see God at work?

How was your faith challenged?

What are you learning about serving?

Why are you thankful for your team?

How can you bless others tomorrow?

DAY FIVE:
the edge heats up

Shadrach, Meshach, and Abednego were just barely teenagers when they were forcefully taken from their homes in Jerusalem to serve in the palace of Nebuchadnezzar, King of Babylon. Babylon was not an easy place for three young Jewish boys to live out their faith. However, Shadrach, Meshach, and Abednego (along with their friend Daniel) had determined to love and serve only the One True God in the midst of all the evil of Babylon.

Read Daniel 3:12-30 (it's a long read, but a great story).

If anyone was ever on "the edge," it was these guys—literally. They stood on the edge of a blazing hot furnace. Behind them was Babylon, ahead of them was a painful death, but inside of them was a deep faith in the God they loved and served. It's obvious in their statement to King Nebucanezzer:

When life heats up, we, understandably, want God to just walk in and put out the flames. But that's not always the way He works.

If we are thrown into the blazing furnace,
the God we serve is able to save us from it,
and he will rescue us from your hand,
O king. But even if he does not,
we want you to know,
O king, that we will not serve your
gods or worship the image of gold
you have set up.
Daniel 3:17-18

They knew God was in control. They knew it would be no problem for him to take out Neb and his men, and set them free. They also knew God might choose to let them die in the furnace, and even bring some good out of their deaths. It's doubtful they ever imagined what actually ended up happening, but it's certain they knew God was capable of doing way more than they could ever imagine.

When life heats up, we, understandably, want God to just walk in and put out the flames. But that's not always the way He works. Sometimes He has us walk right through the fire because He has even greater things in mind than we can comprehend.

What sort of response does the King have to the miracle in the furnace?

What kind of reaction would you like people to have when they see you living "on the edge?"

What are some expectations that you have of God right now? Things you're counting on him to accomplish or provide?

Are you able to trust God, "even if he doesn't?"

"We who have Christ's eternal life
need to throw away our own lives."
- George Verwer

today···

How did you see God at work?

How was your faith challenged?

What needs is God calling you to respond to?

What made you laugh?

How can you bless others tomorrow?

DAY SIX:
not mine but yours

Let the morning bring me word of your unfailing love,
for I have put my trust in you.
Show me the way I should go, for to you I lift up my soul.
Psalm 43:8

You're surrendering to the all-wise, all-powerful, sovereign God of the universe who loves and cares for you more deeply than you can comprehend.

God invites us to come and follow Him. Its way more than just asking Him to forgive our sins and "come into our heart." It's walking with Him right now, step by step, day by day. It's an invitation to adventure for certain, but it's also an invitation to surrender. Surrender isn't something we like to talk about. It makes us think of losing, giving up, and not getting our way…things that, in general, never go over well with the human race.

But surrendering to Jesus puts a different spin on things. Surrendering to Him means surrendering to His will and rule in our lives, which Romans 12:2 describes as "good, pleasing and perfect." You're not surrendering to some psycho dictator or power hungry control freak. You're surrendering to the all-wise, all-powerful, sovereign God of the universe who loves and cares for you more deeply than you can comprehend.

Let's spend the rest of today looking at a moment in Jesus' life that led to the ultimate act of love and surrender.

Read and think about Mark 16:32-39 and Jesus' final hours before the cross.

How would you describe what Jesus is feeling and experiencing in these verses?

What did He ask of God?

What statement of surrender does Jesus make in verse 36?

Did you get that? "Not my will but yours." Just hours before his very human body would experience torture beyond what we can imagine, Jesus begs God to somehow get him out of it, but his prayer doesn't end there…he surrenders. He says no to his flesh and yes to God.

"Not my will but yours."

Do something today to get that statement of surrender etched in your heart and mind. Write it over and over again until all the white on this page is filled. Say it over and over again until someone looks at you strange, then start saying it louder! Repeat it until you start to grasp it's meaning and are sure that you trust God enough to surrender. You'll be transformed when those words become your sincere prayer.

It (faith) is the change from being confident about our own efforts to the state in which we despair of doing anything for ourselves and leave it to God.
C.S. Lewis, Mere Christianity

today···

How did you see God at work?

How was your faith challenged?

What are you thankful for?

What's been the hardest comfort from home to do without?

How can you bless others tomorrow?

DAY SEVEN:

getting your feet wet

Living by faith isn't usually the nice and neat little package we'd like it to be. Others might misunderstand us. We might not understand what God's doing. Faith can, many times, end up being kind of messy. For Peter, faith was not only messy, it was soaking wet.

A life lived on the edge often means taking a leap into unknown territory with an unknown outcome.

Peter is an interesting guy to study up on. Seeing his faith evolve from a rough fisherman to a radical disciple of Christ can teach us all a ton about the way God works and the people God uses. Today we're going to focus on one of the many defining moments Peter had after he answered Jesus' call to follow Him.

Read and think about Mathew 14:26-31.

How would you describe Peter's faith in this story?

What set his faith apart from the other's in the boat?

What do you learn about Jesus' from his part in the story?

A life lived on the edge often means taking a leap into unknown territory with an unknown outcome. It means leaving what's comfortable and getting your feet wet. Peter was far from perfect, but at least he got out of the boat, and for the briefest moment, Peter did the impossible: *he walked on water.* And in a moment of crisis, Peter learned first hand that Jesus is there to catch us when our faith wavers.

What would it look like for you to "get out of the boat" today?

Spend some time talking to God about any fears or concerns you have about "getting out of the boat," then spend some time listening to His response.

So do not fear, for I am with you;
do not be dismayed, for I am your God.
I will strengthen you and help you;
I will uphold you with my righteous right hand.
Isaiah 41:10

today...

How did you see God at work?

How was your faith challenged?

What are you going to miss when you leave?

What made you laugh?

How can you bless others tomorrow?

DAY EIGHT:
with all your heart

Have you ever read from the Amplified version of the Bible? To help the reader better grasp the true meaning of a passage of scripture, it will include additional words that expand on an idea or thought. For example, you might say to your friend, *"Would you like to go out for lunch?"* The Amplified version of that question would be something like, *"Would you like, wish or desire to go out, away from home, to a restaurant, for lunch, a light meal in the middle of the day?"* Do you get the idea?

Today we're going to do some of our own amplification of a couple verses of scripture.

Read and think about the following verses:

> *Trust in the Lord with all your heart,*
> *and lean not on your own understanding;*
> *In all your ways acknowledge Him,*
> *and he will make your paths straight.*
> *Proverbs 3:5-6*

These are some classic verses about trusting God. They've been written on plaques and hung on walls. They've been printed on greeting cards and given to high school graduates along with a ten dollar bill. Why? Because the truths they contain are great advice for anyone seeking to live by faith.

Take some time now to pull these verses apart and "amplify" them. In the space after each phrase, re-write it in your own words, describing what it may mean anyway you can. The first one is started for you.

TRUST:
Rely on, put your faith in, follow no matter how crazy it may seem…

IN THE LORD:

WITH ALL YOUR HEART:

AND LEAN NOT:

ON YOUR OWN UNDERSTANDING:

IN ALL YOUR WAYS:

ACKNOWLEDGE HIM:

AND HE:

WILL MAKE YOUR PATHS STRAIGHT:

How do you think God wants you to apply this verse to your life today?

Trust in him at all times, O people;
pour out your hearts to him,
for God is our refuge.
Psalm 62:8

today...

How did you see God at work?

How was your faith challenged?

Who is a new friend you've made on this trip?

What are you looking forward to about home?

How can you bless others tomorrow?

DAY NINE:

peace on the edge

Now may the Lord of peace himself give you peace
at all times and in every way.
The Lord be with all of you.
2 Thessalonians 4:16

Peace comes in situations completely surrendered to the sovereign authority of Christ.

Fear. Hesitancy. Doubting. Sometimes being on the edge is just like that feeling you get at the top of a hill on a roller coaster: excitement, terror, anticipation and nausea all rolled into one as your stomach leaps up to your throat and even the toughest man can't help but let a scream escape. But, there's something else that can be found on the edge. Something you wouldn't expect to find in such a precarious position, but something you welcome when it finds you: PEACE. It's who Jesus is. It's what He offers us.

Inexplicable PEACE.

When our path is uncertain: PEACE.

When our safety is threatened: PEACE.

When life seems out of control: PEACE.

When we face an impossible challenge: PEACE.

Look at Isaiah 9:6-7:

> *For to us a child is born, to us a son is given.*
> *And the government will be on his shoulders.*
> *And he will be called Wonderful Counselor,*

Mighty God, Everlasting Father,
PRINCE OF PEACE.
Of the increase of his government and peace there will be no end.
He will reign on David's throne and over his kingdom.
Establishing and upholding it with justice and righteousness
from that time on and forever.
The zeal of the Lord will accomplish this.
(emphasis added)

Peace is mentioned a couple of times in this passage, and so are things relating to authority, reign and government. So what's the connection? Beth Moore, in "Living Free," says this:

> The key to peace is authority. When we allow the Prince of Peace to govern our lives, peace either immediately or ultimately results. Peace accompanies authority. Peace comes in situations completely surrendered to the sovereign authority of Christ.

When we stop trying figure out and fix everything, and surrender it all to Jesus, it opens the door for peace to come. When we acknowledge that Jesus is in control and we're not, peace accepts the invitation to come and fill us up.

Read and think about the following verses that also talk about peace. Re-write each one in your own words and then journal any other insights God gives you into the peace found in Him.

Isaiah 26:3

Philippians 4:6-7

John 14:1, 27

You will keep in perfect peace him whose mind is steadfast,
because he trusts in you. Trust in the Lord forever,
for the Lord, the Lord, is the Rock eternal.
Isaiah 26:-4

today...

How did you see God at work?

How was your faith challenged?

Who is going to be hardest to say good-bye to ?

What have you learned about putting others first?

How can you bless others tomorrow?

DAY TEN:
help on the edge

The Apostle Paul is responsible for writing nearly half of the books of the New Testament. When you read words of scripture like, "to live is Christ, to die is gain," and "I rejoice in what was suffered for you," you get a good picture of just how passionate He was about following Christ. Such a good picture, in fact, that's it's easy to forget what a dramatic event his coming to believe in Jesus was, and the total 180° flip his life took after Jesus laid him out flat on a dusty road to Damascus.

Let's refresh our memories and read Acts 9:1-19.

Two chapters earlier (Acts 7), Saul (later Paul) was looking on with approval as Stephen, the first Christian martyr, met his death. Verse one of chapter nine makes it clear that Saul wasn't planning on stopping at the death of one follower of Christ. He was out for blood. But then God steps in as only God can do, and Saul becomes Paul, one of the most radical followers of Christ the world has ever seen.

Now, look at the role of Ananias in the story.

What do you think he must have been feeling when he got his directions from God to help Saul?

How do his actions show that he trusted God?

Look a bit further into chapter 9 at verses 26-28.

Ananias and Barnabas stuck their necks pretty far out on behalf of Paul. Scripture doesn't expand on it too much, but we can imagine that it probably wasn't an easy thing to do. It was probably more out of obedience than desire that they came to the aid of the murderer of one of their fellow believers. Barnabas and Ananias trusted that the Lord knew what he was doing, even when it may have seemed like a set up to meet the same fate as Stephen. Their example helped introduce another man to "edge living," and Paul, in turn, has challenged countless others to join them there in that place of radical faith and trust.

Is there anyone God is asking you to reach out to, as Ananias and Barnabas reached out to Saul?

Spend some time asking God to give you the faith and courage to do it.

"But I tell you: Love your enemies
and pray for those who persecute you."
Matthew 5:44

today...

How did you see God at work?

How was your faith challenged?

What are you thankful for?

What made you laugh?

How can you bless others tomorrow?

END OF TRIP
debrief

Taking some time to reflect on your trip is essential to letting it become a life-changing experience. Answer the following questions to help you process all that you've seen and experienced. If possible, share your answers with your teammates before your trip is over, or with a good friend when you get home.

What characteristic of God was most evident to you during your trip? How?

What was the biggest thing you learned about God and how he works?

In what ways were you stretched and pushed out of your comfort zone?

What did you learn about being part of a team?

What did you appreciate most about your team members?

What was your favorite part of ministry? Where did you see yourself excel?

Where did you see the need for change in yourself?

How did your thinking about the poor and needy change?

What did you learn about other cultures?

Who was the person (non-team member) that impacted you most? How?

What changes do you hope people will see in you when you return home?

How can you continue to be involved in ministry and meeting the needs of others at home?

Check out the ideas for staying involved in missions on page 67.

DAY ELEVEN:
love takes a risk

When Paul was still Saul he prided himself in being the "perfect" Jew. He ran in the right circles, said and did all the right things, and obeyed the law better than anyone else. Jewish law covered almost every area of life, and there were many laws about what was considered "clean" and "unclean." There were strict rules about what could not be eaten and what could not be touched in order to avoid becoming "unclean." Everyone who wasn't a Jew was called a Gentile, and because they didn't observe the same laws as the Jews, much of what they did and who they were was considered horribly unclean. This caused a huge divide of prejudice between the two groups of people.

God wants you to take a leap of faith and love those the world has rejected.

Imagine what a shock it must have been when the once devout Jew, was called to bring the Good News of salvation through Jesus Christ to the Gentiles (Galatians 2:7). He might as well have been called to go touch radioactive waste—the prejudice was that severe.

We don't know what Paul thought initially when he received his calling, but scripture gives us no evidence that he resisted in any way. Jesus had taken hold of Paul's life, and changed him in every way from the inside out. The once elite and haughty Jew was willing to lay it all down so that *everyone* could be reached with the Good News that had done such a transforming work in his life. What others thought didn't matter.

Read and think about Philippians 3:4-13 and 4:12-13.

What do you think Paul had learned that gave him the compassion and desire to minister to a people that many of his peers would have considered grossly unclean?

Who are the "hard to love" people in your life?

Who are the people who, if you started loving them with the love of Jesus, would cause many to cringe?

God wants you to take a leap of faith and love those the world, and sadly even sometimes the church, has rejected. He wants you to risk rejection yourself to bring the Good News to *all* people *everywhere*.

Spend some time praying, asking God to give you a heart of compassion and love for those who may be hard to love, but are in such desperate need of the hope of Christ.

...if you spend yourselves in behalf of the hungry and
satisfy the needs of the oppressed,
then your light will rise in the darkness,
and your night will become like the noonday.
Isaiah 58:10

today...

How did you see God at work?

How was your faith challenged?

What surprised you about coming home?

How do you see that you have changed?

How can you bless others tomorrow?

DAY TWELVE:

what we cannot see

Faith is being sure of what we hope for,
and certain of what we do not see.
Hebrews 11:1

Again, God uses our sense of sight to shed light on what walking by faith really is. Hebrews chapter 11 is an awesome look at a whole string of people who lived their lives on the edge. They didn't grow up and get a nice job and find a nice neighborhood to build a nice house filled with nice things. They spent their time here on earth living on the edge, and God used them in mighty, mighty ways.

Look further into Hebrews 11, specifically at verses 10, 13-15.

How do these verses help shed light on what verse 1 is talking about?

What were the people in these verses hoping for?

What couldn't they see?

Hebrews 11 also records the many hardships these heroes of the faith endured.

Read Hebrews 11:36-38

How do you think their hope of a future heavenly homeland helped them make it through?

This world isn't all there is. In fact, this world is just a blip on the grand timeline of eternity. When we start to really live like this world is temporary and eternity is forever, it will change us in huge ways. That's what happened to the people named in Hebrews 11. They were certain that God had them on a journey with a phenomenal final destination. It made the things that so often consume our time, energy, and thoughts seem not so important any more. It made them see that the things that really matter on this earth are the things that will endure for eternity.

> When we start to really live like this world is temporary and eternity is forever, it will change us in huge ways.

What are some things going on in your life right now that are a big deal for you?

How does your hope of a heavenly homeland change your perspective on the situation?

Walking by faith is living in a reality not yet seen.
Relying on sight—as paradoxical as it sounds—
blinds us to God's best.
--Jennifer Rothschild, Walking by Faith

today...

How did you see God at work?

How was your faith challenged?

What ways can you serve at home?

What are you trusting God for?

How can you bless others tomorrow?

DAY THIRTEEN:

more than you can imagine

God has a knack for keeping us guessing. So often He'll show us just enough to take the next step, and not much past that. But maybe it's not so much that God wants to "keep us guessing," as that He wants to keep us *trusting.* Walking a path that is *uncertain*, tends to make us *certain* of what God desperately wants us to be sure of: WE CAN TRUST HIM.

Spend some time reading and thinking about the verses below.

> And I pray that you, being rooted and established in love,
> may have power, together with all the saints, to grasp how wide
> and long and high and deep is the love of Christ,
> and to know this love that surpasses knowledge that you may be
> filled to the measure of all the fullness of God.
> Now to him who is able to do immeasurably more
> than all we ask or imagine,
> according to his power that is at work within us,
> to him be glory in the church
> and in Christ Jesus throughout all generations,
> for ever and ever! Amen.
> Ephesians 3:17-21

> "No eye has seen, no ear has heard, what God has prepared for
> those who love him."
> 1 Corinthians 2:9

When our path seems uncertain, we can be certain that we can trust God.

What else do these verses show we can know for sure about the path God has for us?

When our path seems uncertain, we can be certain that we can trust God.

Maybe God doesn't always reveal much of what's next because we wouldn't believe Him if He did!

End today by spending some time praying, surrendering yourself to God's will and rule in your life, no matter how unimaginable it may be.

If the Lord delights in a man's way, he makes his steps firm;
though he stumble, he will not fall,
for the Lord upholds him with his hand.
Psalm 37:23-24

today···

How did you see God at work?

How was your faith challenged?

What has been hardest about being home?

How has your trip changed the way you love others?

How can you bless others tomorrow?

mission trip ideas & tips

PACKING

- Packing your things in large zip-lock bags with all the air squeezed out helps save room in your bag, and keeps you organized while traveling.
- Take everything out of its packaging (toiletries, medicines, etc.) to save space. If you need to, just cut the directions off the packaging and put them in a zip-lock with the item.
- No matter how hot it is where you are going, bring at least one long-sleeve shirt. You never know when you might get stuck on a freezing cold plane, or when you'll need protection from bugs, etc.
- If you're flying to your location, pack some extra clothes in your carry-on because your luggage might not arrive with you.
- Earplugs are great to have along if you're sleeping in a noisy place or in a room with people who snore!
- Bring pictures of your family, friends, etc. Family ties are generally stressed more in other cultures than in the U.S., so people will love seeing pictures of your relatives! Try not to bring photos that would show off your comparative "wealth," or show you dressed inappropriately for the culture you will be visiting.
- A small supply of powdered Gatorade can be great to have along, to help guard against dehydration, if you're going to a hot location. Keep a zip-lock bag of it in your backpack and sneak some into your water bottle once in a while.
- If you're going overseas and will be able to make phone calls home, make sure to find out the international access codes for pre-paid phone cards beforehand. You can usually find this out by calling the customer service number on the back of your card.

- Traveler's checks are not recommended for short trips. Most stores will not accept them. Finding a bank that cashes them and getting you to the bank can be a hassle for your team. Cash is best, but ask your team leaders what they recommend.

CULTURE

- Get ready to be flexible. Things in other cultures don't run on tight schedules, as things in the States usually do. Make use of the "waiting" time you're sure to have. Use the time to get to know your teammates better, or nationals who may be with you. Keep a book with you to pull out during these times. Choose some Scripture to memorize and work on it while you wait.
- Greetings are very important in many cultures. Find out ahead of time or learn what the appropriate greetings are as soon as you arrive, then put them into practice.
- Remember that common body language in the States may mean something totally different in the culture where you are going. For example, our common "okay" sign is seen as inappropriate in many Latin countries.
- If they speak another language where you are going, make sure to learn a few phrases beforehand. Learning the phrase, "How do you say…" can be very useful, along with some pointing, to pick up words and phrases once you arrive.
- Make sure to pay attention to any dress-code guidelines you may have been given for the culture you are visiting. Dressing appropriately can really have an affect on how people treat you.
- In many cultures, showing respect to those older than you is very important.
- Hospitality can look different in other cultures. Our family-style way of serving meals and serving yourself isn't common in other countries. If you're going to be eating meals prepared by nationals, be ready to have a full plate of food set in front of you, and be ready to eat it! Put aside any picky eating habits during your trip.
- It's best not to pull out your camera during the first couple of days of your trip. Wait until people know you a little better. Ask

before you take people's pictures, and be sensitive to those who don't want their picture taken. Don't make people feel like they are part of your sightseeing tour.

- Don't make promises you won't keep about staying in touch with people or sending them things, etc. Sometimes even mentioning something as a possibility, "maybe I can send you some clothes," is understood as a promise.
- Long church services in languages you don't understand can be killers! To help pass the time, try to at least pick out what passage of Scripture is being taught and spend time reading and meditating on it. Also, let everything be a cue to pray! Pray for the pastor as he preaches. During worship, pray that God would be glorified in the service. If a child cries, pray that he/she would grow up to love and serve the Lord. If a chicken runs through, pray that God would provide adequate food for the community.

WORKING WITH YOUR HOSTS

- Appreciate the people who are hosting you on your mission trip! Many times they are taking time away from their normal jobs, or adding onto their normal work schedule to make your trip happen.
- Be careful not to bombard your host with questions about what's going on, the schedule, etc. They are in charge of a lot and probably getting more questions than they need. Run questions like that through your team leader.
- The local missionaries or church where you may be working will be there long-term. Be intentional about inviting people to their church, and introducing people from the church to people you build relationships with. If you're doing a Bible school for children, or any sort of meetings, try to get your hosts involved, so that people see them and not just the foreigners.
- Bring a small gift for your host, if your team leader thinks it's appropriate. Think of special ways your team can serve them. If you have time in your schedule, you could wash their cars, treat them to a special meal, or watch their children while they have a night out.

GIVING THINGS AWAY

If you are going to a place where people are living in poverty, you're probably going to be asked for things, and you are probably going to want to give to help meet the need. Giving is good, but has to be done carefully or it can cause more damage than good. Make sure your giving is done appropriately.

- Be careful about not giving things in a way that will create jealousy or cause fighting. If you give your watch to a child, all the others will want it and it may be stolen.
- It is best not to give away money to people. It may not be used for the purpose you intend. Also, if children who are begging make enough money doing it, parents may not think it is worthwhile to send the children to school, etc.
- If you want to give away your clothes or other items, ask your team leader or host for the best way to do so. Your host probably knows the needs of the community best, and they can help make sure your donation goes where it's needed most.
- Be aware that giving away donations can be a lot of work for others. Don't assume that your host wants that responsibility. It's not that they don't want to help meet needs, they may just not have time to spend dealing with your donations. For example, clothes that are left often need to be washed and sorted before they can be given away.

MINISTRY

Almost anything can be turned into a creative ministry tool and open up a chance for you to talk to someone. If there is something you can do that you think may be of use during your trip, ask your team leader to find out if it would be appropriate where you are going.

Here are a few ideas to get your mind thinking:

- Magic tricks/optical illusions, juggling, etc., always seem to draw a crowd.

- A bag of fingernail polish can come in handy, if you're working with youth, visiting a nursing home, a hospital, etc. Give some free manicures!
- Do you know how to cut hair? Bring along some scissors or a pair of clippers and set up a barbershop. Especially in poorer areas, haircuts may be rare for some people.
- Can you draw? Keep a drawing pad in your backpack and pull it out to entertain people. You can draw something and have someone tell you how to say it in the local language. If you're visiting a hospital, you can draw people's names or a verse and hang your work above their beds to brighten things up.
- Do you like to take pictures? Some people never get a family photo taken. Setting up a mobile photo studio can be a great ministry. If you have a Polaroid camera, you can give them the photos right away. Otherwise, you may be able to find a one-hour photo shop that can get you your pictures fast. Make sure to check on how/if the logistics of this will work in your location.
- Women love to make things. If you're going to have a chance to lead a womens' or girls' Bible study, think of a simple craft to have them do as well. Canvas bags work well for this. You can either buy them at a craft store or make them yourself. Have women decorate them using ribbon, buttons, rubber stamps and fabric paint, etc.
- Making journals can also be a great thing to do with youth or adults. Bring along enough of the "composition" style notebooks (no coil binding) for the people you will be working with. You can make fabric covers and decorate them. Or, have them make a collage on the cover by cutting things out of old magazines and calendars and coating them with modge-podge glue. After making the journals, you can talk about how to use them for their daily quiet time. Print out a list of tips for having a daily quiet time and glue it on the inside cover, or write Scripture references on each page for them to look up during their personal quiet time with the Lord.

APPENDIX II

ideas for staying
involved in missions

INTERNET RESOURCES:

www.thetravelingteam.org
This is a great web-site geared towards college students with tons of ideas and resources for staying involved in missions around the world.
www.globalprayerdigest.org and www.joshuaproject.net
Both of these websites include the latest information on where the greatest needs for the gospel are around the world. Sign up for daily prayer emails to keep you involved in praying for the nations!

THINGS TO DO:

- **PRAY!!!** Just because you've left the mission field doesn't mean you have to stop interceding for the needs of the location you were in. Buy a map of the place you visited, decorate it with pictures of the people you ministered to and use it as a prayer reminder. The internet resources listed above have great resources for praying for the nations.
- **Get involved with internationals in your area.** Universities often have programs to connect with international students on campus. You can show them around and help them get adjusted to their new environment or invite them over for a meal during the holidays when they are far from family.
- **Read missionary biographies** to learn more about taking the gospel to the nations. There are tons of great stories out there that will inspire your faith in God and love for all people.

- **Learn another language.** Let your love for people of other cultures be what motivates you to learn!
- **Support a missionary.** There are missionaries all over the world who are in need of whatever you can give financially. They're also in need of prayer and encouragement that you can give.
- **Get involved in the missions committee at your church.** Churches always need people to help them care for the missionaries they support and to get others involved in missions.
- **Give to missions projects around the world.** There are projects that bring Bibles, fresh water, and food to people that don't have them. There are orphanages, Bible schools, homeless shelters…the needs are endless!
- **Get involved with the poor and needy where you are at.** Volunteer at a homeless shelter or an after school kids program. Pack food at your local food bank. There are people right where you're at with needs you can help meet.